DOCK LEAVES

Hugo Williams was born in Windsor in 1942 and grew up in Sussex. He worked on the *London Magazine* from 1961 to 1970, since when he has earned his living as a journalist and travel writer (*No Particular Place To Go*, 1980). He was TV critic on the *New Statesman* and theatre critic on the *Sunday Correspondent*. He is currently film critic for *Harper's & Queen* and writes the 'Freelance' column in the *TLS*. He lives in London.

by the same author

WRITING HOME (O.U.P.)
SELECTED POEMS (O.U.P.)
SELF-PORTRAIT WITH A SLIDE (O.U.P.)

Dock Leaves HUGO WILLIAMS

faber and faber

LONDON · BOSTON

First published in 1994
by Faber and Faber Limited
3 Queen Square, London, WC1N 3AU

Photoset by Wilmaset Ltd
Printed in England by Clays Ltd, St Ives plc.

© Hugo Williams, 1994

Hugo Williams is hereby identified as the author of
this work in accordance with Section 77 of the
Copyright, Designs and Patents Act 1988.

A CIP record for this book
is available from the British Library.

ISBN 0-571-17175-3

10 9 8 7 6 5 4 3 2 1

In Memory of My Mother
Margaret Vyner 1914–1993

Contents

ACKNOWLEDGEMENTS

Some of these poems have appeared in the *Guardian*, *Independent on Sunday*, *London Magazine*, *London Review of Books*, *New Review*, *New Writing*, *The New Yorker*, *Observer*, *Poetry Review*, *Sunday Times*, *Times Literary Supplement* and the BBC *Bookmark* film *Love in a Cold Climate*. I would like to thank Neil Rennie for his great help over the years.

On Our Marks

I start furthest back
on the yew tree path, crouching down,
my fingers touching the earth.
My brother comes next,
just far enough ahead to give me a race.
Our sister, nearest home,
looks over her shoulder at us,
knowing she will probably win.

At the end of the path you stand,
one hand holding up a yellow handkerchief.
We wait on our marks,
our hearts beating faster now, our eyes
fixed on your upraised hand,
the handkerchief fluttering in the wind.

Post-War British

Everyone screwing up their eyes
as if they can't quite make us out –
Jim with his hair fully restored,
Johnny with the Simoniz duster,
polishing the Jowett Javelin to extinction
as long ago as 1951.

There's no such person as Anne,
but Gar is still there, looking quite like
her old self again, and Mr Burns,
none the worse for New Zealand,
waiting for us to make up our minds:
are we coming with them or not?

The afternoon goes on like that
until we are piling into the car,
trying not to sit in the middle.
Isn't that the anti-carsick chain
hanging down behind, that was supposed to
earth the static electricity?

It doesn't even touch the ground!
The children leaning out of the windows
must be waving goodbye
to their own grandchildren,
but they think they can smell the sea
just over the next horizon.

And here we all are at last —
our faces coming up tired but satisfied
at the other end of our lives,
our knitted bathing-trunks falling down.
The cross-hatched anti-invasion groynes
postmark the scene for us

and all the dogs that existed then,
named after Sid Field characters,
leaping to within an inch of the stick
that hovers in the air above the sea,
bring it back to us now
and lay it at our feet.

A Dam

My mother calls my name,
a familiar, two-note sound
that carries across the fields
and finds me here,
kneeling beside a stream,
my arms plunged up to the elbows in mud.

I make my way back to the house
and try to explain
what I've been doing all this time
so far away from home.
'Making dams?' she will ask.
'Or making poems about making dams?'

Standstill

*A last visit to the long-abandoned 'Gosses' on Harold Macmillan's
Birch Grove estate, soon to be levelled as part of a new golf course.*

I apologize to the driver
for the branches closing in,
almost bringing us to a standstill.
He doesn't seem to mind.
'I'm like you,' he tells me, as we move aside
a tree blown across the drive by the storm.
'I had to come back home
to see my own particular corner of the UK
before I died. Our daughter wanted to stay out there
in New Zealand and get married.
Don't ask me why.
She's a karate champion.'

We have turned a corner in the drive, past the swing,
past the gibbet, past the tree
where we buried the screaming idol's head
of Elsie Byers, the American agent.
Flowering creepers and bushes
crowd round the old house,
as if some great party were being given there
long ago, the party of the season.
Look, the same door! The same knocker!
The same doorhandle I held
when I came back from going round the world!
The same footscraper!

The driver seems to share my astonishment
that everything is the same yet different

when you look through a window
into your old room
and see your head lying there on the pillow,
innocent of your life, but dreaming your dreams.
'Where is it you say old Supermac used to live?
I want to see the field
where President Kennedy landed in his helicopter.
I was cheering and waving the American flag.
Our daughter had just been born. We were on our way
to start a new life in New Zealand.'

Margaret Vyner

1925. Paris passes from high Anglophilia to unbridled Negro-mania. The Charleston is born. Women bob their hair, smoke cigarettes, embark on love affairs. The couturier Jean Patou creates three new scents to evoke the three great moments of love: 'Amour Amour', 'Que Sais-Je?, 'Adieu Sagesse'. On the other side of the world, in Winona, Sydney, a skinny eleven-year-old girl called Margaret Vyner walks through a plate glass window and amazes everyone by escaping unhurt.

1927. Lindbergh crosses the Atlantic. The Surrealist Gallery opens in Paris. From a boutique on the beach at Deauville, Jean Patou launches 'le sportswear'. He dresses tennis star Suzanne Lenglen. The suntanned look is *à la mode* and Patou is the first to introduce suntan oil to the world. It is called 'Chaldée'. In Australia, outdoor girl Margaret Vyner enters Ascham School for Girls, where the uniform is a disappointing beige, like everyone's permanently tanned skin.

1929. Diaghilev dies. Black Friday on Wall Street. For Paris society it is the high summer of ostentation and elegant extravagance. The last wave of desperate optimism inspires Patou's homage in perfume to a generation: 'Moment Suprême'. A gawky fifteen, Margaret Vyner is attending the dancing classes of Alexei Dolinoff, who came to Australia with Pavlova and also teaches Robert Helpmann. Her only despair is that she has grown too tall to be a ballet dancer.

1930. Gandhi comes to Europe. Picasso is awarded the Carnegie Prize. René Clair shoots the first talkie on the roofs of Paris. In the salons of Patou's *hotel particulier* in the Rue St Florentin, a cocktail bar has been opened for the benefit of customers. In recognition of the new decade's sophistication, he has mixed his 'Cocktail' range of scents, bright and fresh as an aperitif. In Sydney, the budding sixteen-year-old is starting to be toasted.

1933. The Bauhaus closes its doors. Pierre Bonnard paints *Le Grand Nu au Miroir*. In America, conserves of pickled rattlesnake go on sale. In Paris, Patou's 'Divine Folie' captures the mood of the moment as one mad craze follows another into oblivion. Margaret Vyner is touring Australia and New Zealand as a chorus girl in the musical comedy *Flora Dora*. *Her* divine folly is a plan to run away to Europe.

1934. Miss Vyner arrives in Paris with no money, no French and no contacts. She attends a Jean Patou dress show for fun and is instantly offered a modelling job by the vigilant couturier. He takes her to dinner in the Bois de Boulogne and then on to the lesbian night-club Le Monocle, where the virginal Australian orders her usual glass of milk.

1935. The liner SS *Normandie* breaks the record for the Atlantic crossing: four days, two hours, twelve minutes. Later the same year, Patou launches his own version of 'Normandie': a spell blended of the sea and the voyage, bound with that special sense of bewildered luxury. Margaret Vyner is photographed in nautical mood at the party to launch the fragrance on board the SS *Normandie* at Cherbourg.

1936. June 19: total eclipse of the sun. Sacha Guitry introduces 'Le Mot de Cambronne' to polite society (General Cambronne is reputed to have uttered '*Merde*' when asked to surrender at Waterloo), while the French government introduces paid holidays to the people. 'Why does the air smell so sweet when I wake in the morning?' Paul Poiret asks Patou. 'What is that subtle flavour of dawn, as if the whole garden has poured into my room?' 'It is the fragrance that has just been created by Patou,' replies Patou. 'And it is called "Vacances".' Margaret Vyner tours his Collection to Lyons, Dijon, Deauville, Biarritz and Cannes. Then flies to Croydon Airport for the next stage of her adventure.

1938. Matisse paints *Le Jardin d'Hiver*. Le Corbusier draws up his plans for the urbanization of Buenos Aires. The skies look threatening over Europe. Rumours of war are mixed with dreams of escape. In this loaded atmosphere, Patou-Prospero summons up his 'Colony' – a scent evocative of sun-ripened fruit and beautiful Creole women in blue-plumed headdresses. In London, our colonial friend has wangled herself the part of someone's girlfriend in a Broadway-bound Freddy Lonsdale play, *Once is Enough*, in order to meet its leading man, Hugh Williams. The first evening on board the SS *Washington*, he sends a note to her table, 'Champagne better than milk. Why don't you join me?' She is soon weaned.

1939. Auden and Isherwood leave England for America. Hugh Williams and Margaret Vyner pawn his mother's mink for a last pre-war holiday on Capri. On September 3 she is sitting in a basket rehearsing Terence Rattigan's *French Without Tears* when she hears the news that war has been declared. The party is over.

1946. Sinatra fever. René Simon opens his acting school in Paris. Death of Gertrude Stein and actor Raimu. Jean Patou's new scent, 'L' Heure Attendue', celebrates the longed-for Liberation with an access of joy for the rebirth of his beloved Paris. On the Left Bank, a new world is stammering into existence. It is the epic poem known as St Germain-des-Prés. On the other side of the Channel, I never go anywhere without my mother's empty Patou scent bottle in the shape of a crown.

The Fall

My father lived in the Garden of Allah,
an exotic, bungalow-style hotel
which Thomas Wolfe told Scott Fitzgerald
he could not believe existed, even in Hollywood.
He was sacked by Paramount after serving only
one year of a five-year contract
when his first three films made the Critics'
Ten Worst Films list for 1934.
He heard the news of his redundancy
when the Studio called him at the Garden
and told him they had 2,400 signed publicity stills
he might like to take home with him.

I found them thirty years later,
stuck together from damp in an old vanity case.
Almost everything about him had changed,
if it ever really existed.
The toothbrush moustache, slightly curled,
recalled the Garden of Allah, long since demolished
by the Lytton Loan and Savings Company
to make way for another tower block.
The Company left behind a model of the Garden
to mark the spot where it had stood on Sunset Blvd.
I went looking for the model in 1975,
but it too had disappeared without trace.

The Phoney War

The Army contrived to enter
a wide range of deductions
for this particular week.
No one got much above ten shillings.
Your father, I remember,
whose debts to the Inland Revenue
amounted to four figures,
received, incredulously, about 8/6.
He had placed the coins on the railway line
and let a train pass over them,
so that they were larger, thinner,
and completely valueless.

                    *

According to the Sergeant Major
he would have been burnt to a cinder
when he set his foot
on the live rail we'd heard so much about,
if it hadn't been for the toe-caps
on his boots, or the fact that
his bayonet was fixed.
Everyone except your father
had some theory or other
why he was lucky to be still alive
guarding Staines Railway Bridge
during the Phoney War.

War and Peace

'The hotel has been opened up as an officers' rest place
and the *boule* table dug up from the cellar.
Nobody to run the thing, so Hugh Fraser and I
borrowed all the ready we could lay our hands on
and started crouping like crazy. Everything was fine
until we got smacked for 800 francs in a single coup.
Ugly moments followed as IOUs were hastily written
and Robin Baring despatched to the camp
to fetch the profits from the men's canteen.
I was terrified and Hugh looked very white and sweaty,
as we had no idea how we could fix the canteen money.
Robin returned and we redeemed our IOU's, then,
by the grace of God, the Navy arrived, determined
to wipe us out. We recouped completely, something like
eleven mille and made about 800 each. Next morning
there was a notice in the Mess: "Until further notice
Officers will not run the bank at Boule."
So we've arranged for the Grenadiers to take it over.'

The war used up the last of my father's winning streak
and sent him home to face the music.
The Inland Revenue were waiting behind the door.
'If you do this to me now,' he told the Tax Inspector,
'I'll leave this bloody country and never come back.'
The following week they took away his passport.
After six years in the Army, looking forward to all this,
he's standing guard by his bedroom window,
keeping watch for the landlord's Jaguar.
He rubs an invisible coin between finger and thumb,
twists his signet ring round and round with circular

reasoning. He would like to slip through the ring
and disappear, but his family is watching and waiting
to see what he will do next. He jumps to his feet
and goes on frantic, all-night house hunting missions
to London on the Green Line bus. He came home one morning
in a taxi, holding up two cards, a jack and a nine,
his winning hand in a game of *chemin de fer*.

Elephants

A mix of feelings came to me
when I saw your father's photograph in the *Guardian*
and read the text of your article.
Warm recollections of Tam as I knew him
in a camp on a hillside in Tunisia,
gratitude at my good fortune in having known him,
then sadness at being told you were only just beginning
to talk to one another when he died.

It was a strong enough mixture to make me write to you.
I shall certainly get your book,
but I wanted to say that as a young officer in Phantom
I met an array of self-confident (outwardly),
able and/or aristocratic young men,
who came from a different world from my own.
I learnt a lot from conversations on politics and philosophy
between Christopher Mayhew and Hugh Fraser,

I watched your father playing backgammon
for what I thought incredible stakes
and my Scottish Presbyterian background was fascinated
and repelled by language and attitudes
that were not mine. Tam's sensitivity to my thoughts,
his courtesy and warmth and unmalicious humour,
made him a sort of serene, poised hero for me,
so different was your apprehension of him.

Just after the surrender of the German army in Tunisia
he and I and another were in Carthage
'emptying the ashtrays and counting the broken glasses'.
Tam did a one-man act of getting elephants

on board ship for Hannibal's expedition to Italy.
One of us pointed out that Hannibal had gone by way of
Tangiers.
Immediately Tam shouted out, 'Cancel, change of orders',
and went through a one-man unloading act quite brilliantly.

Last Goodbyes

On the last day of the holidays
we are dying men,
remembering our lost youth
in the rhododendron trees.
We say goodbye to the henhouse,
the potting shed, the flat roof,
the island with a drawbridge.
We have our last go on the swing
with the table underneath
for launching ourselves off into space.
We swing in a great circle,
pushing ourselves away from the tree
with our feet, till we spin
giddily back to the table again –
all afternoon, till it is time to go.
On the last day of the holidays
we stand completely still,
waiting for the taxi to come,
remembering our lost youth
in the rhododendron trees.

The Age of Steam

Remember porters? Weatherbeaten old boys
with watery blue eyes
who were never around when you wanted them?
You had to find one
before you could go anywhere in 1953.
It was part of saying goodbye.
Quick, darling, run and find a porter
while I get your ticket.
I'll meet you at the barrier.

I run off across the station forecourt
in a series of sudden dashes,
panicky knight moves
which leave my head spinning
as I glance over my shoulder at my trunk.
Inside are my darts, my throwing-knife set,
my signalling torch, my *True Romance* magazines –
everything I need to survive
in the months ahead, even my compass.

There are no porters anywhere,
only JADS, assistant head,
standing over by the barrier,
jingling the change in his pocket.
Report to the Master-on-Duty.
Collect your sheets.
Put away your things on the right shelf.

My mother appears like a new sun
from behind a cloud. She is smiling now,
as if to welcome me home.
She has a porter in tow.
I won't wait, darling.
You know how I hate goodbyes.
You've got your comics and your cars.
I've written to you . . .

A last gasp of *Moment Suprême*
as she leans over me, then nothing at all
but the ribbon of her smell unravelling,
the station clock moving on with a little jerk,
the whistle blowing.

This is it, then – the great leap backwards
into make-believe, the covered wagons
drawn in a circle on the dusty plain,
flaming tomahawks flying through the air.

Joy

Not so much a sting
as a faint burn

not so much a pain
as the memory of pain

the memory of tears
flowing freely down cheeks

in a sort of joy
that there was nothing

worse in all the world
than stinging nettle stings

and nothing better
than cool dock leaves.

Lights Out

We're allowed to talk for ten minutes
about what has happened during the day,
then we have to go to sleep.
It doesn't matter what we dream about.

A Blockage

Can you write a letter
saying I don't have to have brawn?
You can see the bristles in it
and pieces of bone.

And can you write a letter
saying when you are coming down?
If you write on Monday
I'll get it on Tuesday

and can use the envelope
to smuggle it out of the dining room.
After supper on Tuesdays
there is a big queue for the lavatories.

Last week there was a blockage
and all the brawn was found
stuck together. When you come down
can we go and see the model village?

Old Boy

Our lesson is really idiotic today,
as if Mr Ray has forgotten
everything he ever knew
about the Reformation
and is making it up as he goes along.

I feel like pointing out
where he's going astray,
but I'm frightened he'll hold up
some of my grey hair
and accuse me of cheating.

How embarrassing
if I turned out to be wrong after all
and Mr Ray was right. Luckily,
I'm in the top class
and come top easily, without trying,
the way it should be.

I could do better
in the written answer questions,
but everyone looks up to me
because I've been round the world
and have my own wife and motorbike.

I'm wearing my old school scarf
that I thought was lost forever.
Brown and magenta quarters,
the smartest colours in the world.
It was round my neck all the time.

Visitants

I went back the other day
to collect my motorbike
from the local police station.
I couldn't believe
that lonely northern outpost
where I went to school
was barely half an hour
from London by train:

not far away and long ago
as I had imagined,
but facing the future
surrounding by Kodak bungalows
and flyovers,
its dreaded Tower
a little spiral staircase
with geraniums in window boxes.

I skidded on the gravel
outside the headmaster's study,
shot round the side
past the library, the Chapel,
the 'Private Side',
hoping to escape without being seen
via the tradesmen's entrance
into Locker's Lane.

Blocking my path,
clipboard and pen at the ready,
stood JADS, brick-faced
Classics master and assistant head,
shouting my name
and bearing down on me,
exactly the same
as when he was alive.

The Accident

The cricket ball lingered an eternity
in the patch of blue sky
before returning eventually to earth.

I was standing with outstretched arms
when the full force of the future
hit me in the mouth.

Man and Superman

A dedicated student of the play –
that was my father's vision
of his start in life. 'When I was your age
I'd seen every play in London.
I read plays for fun.
I queued half way down the Strand
to see Barrymore and du Maurier
in *Man and Superman*.
I sat in the gallery
with the book open on my knee . . .'

It didn't happen that way.
His widowed mother
was a Gallery First Nighter
who took him along with her
to all the popular
star vehicles of the day
and told him he was handsome.
He failed the Army Exam
and went to RADA for a year
to meet women.

When I spun my line
about wanting to do the same
he hit the roof. 'I suppose you think
you'd be famous overnight
and make pots of money. Well, you might.
But then again you might not.
It's my job to think of things like that.
Tell me honestly,
how many plays in London
have you actually seen?'

I clenched my fists under the table
and muttered something about television.
I didn't want to work.
I wanted to make him laugh.
I wanted to make him choke.
I told the one about the constipated airman
and said the last thing first
and had to start again.
His lip came out. His jaw went slack.
'It's rather unfunny, isn't it?'

I'm Your Father, Remember?

I used to think he was naturally like that –
imperious, categorical, always in the wrong
and rightly so, the only man in the world
who could talk about opera and French mustard
as if they were the same sort of thing,
banging the table, saying 'Come off it, old boy!
I'm your father, remember?' – clapping his hands
and when a waiter busied round his chair, saying
'Steady on, you're not a knife-thrower.
Now go out to the kitchen and start again.'
When I stole a comb from the Gentlemen's in the Savoy
he made me take it back. If I'd only murdered
the attendant, all would have been forgiven.
I used to think he was naturally like that.

Four Plays by Hugh and Margaret Williams

1

My mother's mink came out of long-term hock
for the first night
of *Plaintiff in a Pretty Hat*.
It's sprinkling of grey hairs
caught the light
in the foyer of the St Martin's
on the cover of *Theatregoer* magazine
for Christmas 1955. Its glow
of new-found confidence signalled an end
to bankruptcy and woe.

2

It would turn up next
as a character
in their only Broadway success,
The Grass is Greener.
An American millionaire
walks through the wrong door
of a stately home
and falls in love with the Countess.
He wants to give her a mink, a wild one,
without her husband (my father)
finding out about their affair.
They hit on the idea
of a cloakroom ticket
found in a taxi,
but the husband turns the tables on them.
The suitcase flies open
and out fall a cricket bat,

three old cricket pads
and a string of flags.
The couple take hold of the string
and start pulling out the flags as
THE CURTAIN FALLS.

3

The mink would earn its grey hairs
at various first nights and premières
throughout the Sixties,
till my parents came up with their
anti-fur-trade comedy,
The Irregular Verb To Love.
Hedda, my father's theatrical wife,
gets herself arrested
for putting a fire-bomb through the letter-box
of a furriers. The mink was obviously
guilty of something, but what?

4

Demoted from love object
to scapegoat, from one
production to the next,
it could hardly attend the première
of its own burning
and went into hiding
as the lining of my father's
'ultimate winter coat' –
the one he wore
for his own last winter, endlessly touring,
waiting to come into London
with *His, Hers and Theirs*, their last

light comedy about divorce.
He would leave it behind
in his dressing room that Spring,
a headless ghost, an exit line,
a pelt on a stick. My mother's mink
has gone back to storage in my father's head.

Early Morning Swim

Every year now you make your face
a little fainter in its vellum photo-frame,
as if you were washing off your make-up with a towel
and catching the last train home.

You have forgotten how to storm
and shout about the place, but not how to gaze
abstractedly over our shoulders into this room
that is not your room any more.

What do you see that we don't see? Why don't you mind
if we are late coming down to breafast,
or we don't ring up as much as we should?
At this distance, your voice grows fainter on the line,

your words harder to catch. With one hand
you shield your eyes from the sun, as if you have decided
to overlook the way we dress to come up to London
or go to the theatre. You can't see me,

but I can see you, walking away from us, throwing back
your shoulders as you breathe the sea air,
pretending not to limp over the rocky ground.
It is early morning, time for our early morning swim.

You lead the way in your towelling dressing-gown
down the alley behind the hotel, us two boys
sleep-walking along behind you, stumbling
and grumbling a little because it is so early.

We don't understand that this could be our last
swim together, our last chance to prove that we are men.
We don't want to go of course, but we do really.
The water will be cold at this time of day.

Truce

I woke in my clothes and made my way
downstairs. The house was quiet,
like the memory of a house. The furniture
was thin, provisional, ranged against the wall.
My father was standing under a light bulb,
eating a sausage dipped in horseradish sauce.
I helped myself to Shredded Wheat and a banana.
We stood on the verandah together
and peed on the daffodils.

Dinner with My Mother

My mother is saying 'Now'.
'Now,' she says, taking down a saucepan,
putting it on the stove.
She doesn't say anything else for a while,

so that time passes slowly, on the simmer,
until it is 'Now' again
as she hammers out our steaks
for Steak Diane.

I have to be on hand at times like this
for table-laying,
drink replenishment
and general conversational encouragement,

but I am getting hungry
and there is nowhere to sit down.
'Now,' I say, making a point
of opening a bottle of wine.

My mother isn't listening.
She's miles away,
testing the sauce with a spoon,
narrowing her eyes through the steam.

'Now,' she says very slowly, meaning
which is it to be,
the rosemary or tarragon vinegar
for the salad dressing?

I hold my breath, lest anything
should go wrong at the last minute.
But now it is really 'Now',
our time to sit and eat.

Algarve, 1991

World Service

Ten to four and the World Service still on upstairs,
which means that you are sleeping well again tonight,
which means that it got you off to sleep
and hasn't yet woken you again. The sound of waves
from the sea at the foot of the cliff
washes over the voices coming and going in waves.
A motor scooter starts up, then fizzles out again.

I can't sleep, so I get up and look out of the window
onto the dim-lit esplanade, where one or two couples
are finding their way home from the clubs.
I feel jealous and sad, but I like to see them,
lingering at discreet intervals under the palm trees.
Out at sea, the last fishing boats are coming in,
their big lamps slung below the horizon like stars.

For a moment, the broadcast voice upstairs
rises above the waves, insistent, incoherent, cracked.
You wake yourself and manage to reach out a hand
to switch it off. 6.30 and the World Service is quiet,
which means that you are sleeping well again tonight.
Far below, the beach tractor ploughs back and forth,
readying the beach for another day.

Algarve, 1992

Holiday Poem

Some little bird near here
is going 'What? What? What?' all the time,
as if he can't understand what I am saying.
O what is the matter little bird?
Why can't you relax for a moment in the sun
the way I am doing, sing a song,
enjoy the day for what it is?
'What? What? What? What? What?'

The sun is out, clouds are flying past on boards,
chickens are pecking at windfalls,
grasshoppers hum. The pears aren't ripe,
but the apple branches are so full of apples
they are being held up by wooden poles.
Why don't you try one?
What harm could it possibly do?
'What? What? What? What? What? What?'

Bird, I am here and you are there
and everything, for the time being at least,
is all right with the world.
You have got the run of your teeth
and I have got a cup of tea, a good book
and someone I love to sit with.
What more could anyone ask?
'What? What? What? What? What? What? What?'

Safe

Remember the days when six things happened every night
and no one wore an overcoat to go out?
Turning your back on a planned evening with friends
you felt the world opening its arms. The triple miracle
of meeting, liking, being liked, was taken for granted
on the way back to her flat.

I feel ashamed tonight, checking the fires are out,
checking the alarm is on, checking the bed is tucked in,
that I am not really old, or ill, or tired,
only sensible. Whatever it is
that goes click-clacking past the end of the street
makes me draw the curtains and call it a rainy night.

Sex

'Sex' seems to be a word that most people understand,
so there is a fair chance that the woman will understand
what the man is getting at when he mentions the subject.

Perhaps he is finding difficulty getting into the passage
and it may be necessary to ask why. Perhaps she is dry
because there is no natural lubricant for the penis,

or perhaps she is very tense and unable to accept him.
It may be that the fault lies with the man, if he cannot
complete the sexual act, or his climax comes too soon.

At this point it may be necessary to enquire about orgasm.
As sexual excitement reaches its climax (orgasm), the man
will recognize that the jerking out of his semen (sperm)

is about to start and that it is inevitable. His semen
is said to be 'coming' and if any discussion is needed
the verb 'to come' may be used without causing offence.

For instance, the woman may be asked if she understands
what the word 'coming' means in this context
and whether she has ever experienced such a thing.

Does she feel herself to be on the verge of 'coming',
only to find herself drawing back from it because of some
unspecified mental problem, and if so, what?

A Look

of 'How could you do this to me?'
was written all over her face,

which he knew very well would soon
be written all over his own.

A Lap of Honour

The front door bangs
and I creep downstairs in my dressing gown,
unable to believe my good luck.
It is like Christmas morning long ago,
the fields all white,
the day like an unopened present.

I can do whatever I like.
I can move the furniture back against the wall.
I can dance a jig in the hall.
I can sit completely still
reading a book about Aristotle.
I can do nothing at all.

Later on, I sit down to supper with myself,
having opened a bottle of wine.
I touch my glass to the TV screen
in a toast to the BBC.
My house is your house, old friend!
Stay switched on all the time if you want to.

With a glass in my hand
I make the tour of my property –
a lap of honour to celebrate my victory.
As I cruise the house, humming to myself,
I set things in motion as I pass,
curtains and cups and kitchen implements

sway to and fro at my touch,
even the chandelier swings back and forth
in cheerful valediction to absent friends.
A birdcage hanging from the ceiling
tolls like a bell
for my new found liberation.

Saturday Morning

Everyone who made love the night before
was walking around with flashing red lights
on top of their heads — a white-haired old gentleman,
a red-faced schoolboy, a pregnant woman
who smiled at me from across the street
and gave a little secret shrug,
as if the flashing red light on her head
was a small price to pay for what she knew.

Prayer

God give me strength to lead a double life.
Cut me in half.
Make each half happy in its own way
with what is left. Let me disobey
my own best instincts
and do what I want to do, whatever that may be,
without regretting it, or thinking I might.

When I come home late at night from home,
saying I have to go away,
remind me to look out the window
to see which house I'm in.
Pin a smile on my face
when I turn up two weeks later with a tan
and presents for everyone.

Teach me how to stand and where to look
when I say the words
about where I've been
and what sort of time I've had.
Was it good or bad or somewhere in between?
I'd like to know how I feel about these things,
perhaps you'd let me know?

When it's time to go to bed in one of my lives,
go ahead of me up the stairs,
shine a light in the corners of my room.
Tell me this: do I wear pyjamas here,
or sleep with nothing on?
If you can't oblige by cutting me in half,
God give me strength to lead a double life.

Static

Meeting again after so long
we scanned our hearts
for the tell-tale static to register.

The impatient scribble of midges
on the evening air?
Or the fine pencil lines of rain?

Faith

After we broke up
and agreed not to call or write
for at least a year,
I found myself drawn
for a little comfort and cheer
not so much to the top shelf
of W. H. Smith
with its flesh-tinted offers
of doom and gloom,

as the bra and knicker counter
of Marks & Spencer,
where row upon row
of carefully labelled
dream-tatters
in chocolate and dusky peach
seemed to encourage
a humorous approach
and faith in a providing world.

Poetry

Ten, no, five seconds
after coming all
over the place
too soon,

I was lying there
wondering
where to put the
line-breaks in.

Message Not Left on an Answerphone

(for C.)

As night comes on, I remember we used to play
at this time of day, and you would tell me:
'Don't get excited now, or we'll miss the film.'
You would be sitting on my lap, making a fuss of me.
A shoulder strap would fall down.
A buckle would come away in my hand.
That famous buckle! Did you get it mended yet?
Sometimes the telephone would ring
while we were playing, making us cross,
even though it was still quite early.
You would pick up the phone and talk noncommittally
for a moment or two, because you had to.
How I loved you when you talked like that.
At other times we let the answerphone do the work
and listened to the names of your friends
coming through from another world.
Darling, we made ourselves late sometimes,
playing those games. We made ourselves cry.
Now it is me who hangs endlessly on the line,
who hears your voice repeating at all hours:
'I can't get to the phone at the moment,
but do leave a message.' Pick up the phone, damn you.
Can't you recognize one of my silences by now?

In the Blindfold Hours

In the blindfold hours,
in the memory wars,
don't fool yourself it never happened,
that you never loved her.
Don't degrade yourself with empty hopes like these.

Go to the window. Listen to the trees.
It is only air we live in.
There is nothing to be frightened of.

Keats

How can I find love in the middle of the night
when the only females out so late
are rag mountains scavenging the bins
behind Indian restaurants? Imagine a dog kennel
made out of old audio cartons. Inside sits a thing
lagged in pink polystyrene, tickling her palm,
blowing out her cheeks at me. She shows me
her business card, an empty sardine tin
attached to a chain round her neck.

I spring forth eagerly, excited by the smell
of sardine oil clinging to her fur. I want to do it
immediately on the pile of old yoghurt pots
and take-away boxes, but she makes me wait
while she slips into something different to go out –
a sheath made of 'I'm Backing Britain' shopping bags,
a veil made of tarred and knotted string.
Like a gigantic hen, she leads the way down Oxford St,
tapping on plate glass windows with a twig.

Special Effects

I see the board with a pencil
for contributions to the flowers
has gone up outside No. 8.
It must be the hairdresser,
the sculptress in lacquer, the part-time
spiritualist who devised her own
special effects – bloodstains and bumps
and lights going on and off
in the upstairs salon
that doubled as a séance chamber.

I used to visit Madame Charmaine
in the long-haired era before last
to have my hair left alone,
my ear bitten by her macaw,
but £10 was a lot of money to pay
for a cup of hairy coffee
and the latest police story
about the runaway daughter
who came at her with a carving knife,
so I stopped going round there.

When she died, a life-sized
papier-maché model was found
sitting with her in the salon.
Its clothes were spattered with theatrical blood.
Its head had been severed.
Madame Charmaine was holding it
in her lap, like a trophy.
Hanks of human hair had been stuck to
the scalp and backcombed
into a sugary helmet like her own.

Soft Porn

Her towel is an island she is cast up on
in attitudes of sleep or abandon,
or screwing up her eyes against the light,
as if she has woken in the middle of the night
and come downstairs to find us all still up
and glanced around her with her mouth quite slack
and fiddled with a catch behind her back.

See how she lowers her body to the sand,
kneeling, with one leg stretched behind,
twisting and turning until she gets it right,
presenting different aspects to our sight,
her sex obscured, in case we had forgotten,
by a picture of itself in cotton,
and now and then a pair of tits all white.

We feel ourselves going down without a fight,
plummeting earthwards from a great height,
but we triumph over it with a loud shout,
walking around with our tummies sticking out,
turning our heads from left to right,
admiring the way the waves go in and out,
and now and then a pair of tits all white.

Holiday's End

1

We leave the villa early, carrying toys,
and drift down to the beach for hangovers.
(There was sand in the bed, one of us didn't sleep.)
Every time we look up, scanning the horizon for a sign,
another package screams behind the mountain,
another sailboard hits the ocean.

A vast departure lounge surrounds us with Duty Free,
Pink Floyd on the seafront p.a., time-share cowboys.
As we lie back, closing our eyes, we are fastening
our seat-belts, putting out our cigarettes, touching down.
The front door we are trying to push open
is snagged with next year's brochures.

2

The treasured routine now briefly no longer treasured,
the long-distance holiday-makers drag their feet
through the stubble fields overhanging the sea.

In the fading light they have left behind a face-mask,
whose curved breathing tubes stick up out of the sand
like the horns of a lost war-helm.

Musical Bumps

Flushed with the success
of 'Young Love'
and his placing in *New Spotlight*'s
Top Ten Band Poll,
Donnie Collins sipped a cool lager
in the reception area
of the Hotel Arcadia, Bray,
and told me frankly:
'More than the Poll,
the most important aspect
of the new disc
is the number of radio plays
it receives – that's the only
real test of a record
and the only true yardstick
by which anyone can measure
the impact of a number.'

Brian Coll, whose cover version
of 'England Swings'
is currently sneaking up
the Irish charts, agreed with him
that radio exposure
can make or break a record.
His 'Ireland Swings'
has all the ingredients
of a monster hit for Brian,
plus a steady demand for it
in the shops. He told me:
'The air of the tune

is sufficiently well known
and the fact that a lot of
towns are mentioned on the disc
gives it a colloquial flavour
which should pay off handsomely.'

2

As everyone knows by now,
Dickie and Rowland Soper
are travelling together
to Luxembourg,
where Dickie will be singing
Ireland's entry
in the Eurovision Song Contest,
with brother Rowland producing.
No one is predicting
just how successful
the lads will be,
but whatever the outcome,
one thing is certain,
back home in Ireland
'Come Back to Stay'
is sure to be one of the year's
biggest sellers
and a moneyspinner
for Rowland and Dickie.
So good luck to them!

3

It isn't easy stepping into your father's shoes
when the shoes in question belong to Jack Ruane.
Yet that is precisely what Jack Junior has done

and Pops is delighted. Of course, Jack Senior
was a household name on the international circuit
long before most of his fans were even born.
From New York to New Ross, from the days of the
foxtrot to the rhythm-and-blues era, he built up
a steady following among the dance-hall crowd,
who never missed one of his Latin American dates
at the Hotel Arcadia. Recently, however, he has been
obliged to give up the band for health reasons
and hand over the reins of leadership to his son,
who has promised to carry on the great tradition.

4

Like most other showbands
The Hoedowners have had their
share of teething troubles
over the years.
The eponymous TV series
which should have
relaunched their career
proved a mixed blessing.
Old wags shook their heads
and predicted the group
would be just another
bunch of also-rans
on the scrapheap of history.

All that has changed.
With their new disc release,
'Showball Crazy',
a bright new star has emerged
and taken his place
alongside the image idols.

His name is Sean Dunphy
and he is a natural.
Now even the knockers have to admit
the ex-carpenter from Co. Clare
has chipped his way
into the ranks
of musical greatness.

5

I've seen them all
in the square jungle
that is the boxing ring
of Dublin's National Stadium,
boxers and singers,
rockers and rollers,
supergroups and no-hopers,
from Gus Farrell to Seamus Dunphy,
from Dickie Rock to Spider Murphy,
but none of them
could hold a candle
to the scintillating Dixies,
the knock-out showband
with the punchy beat.

It was the occasion
of *New Spotlight*'s
promotion of the show
to aid the Central Remedial Clinic
and it was a sell-out.
Ballads and blues we had in full
and I liked them all.
Mary Flynn and Mary Byrne,
the Wolfe Tones were there

with Father Joseph on drums.
The Creatures impressed
with their spirited antics.
The Action had their
followers out in force.

Murty Quinn and Chris Grace
highlighted the first half
with their great rendition
of 'Nothing to Lose'.
The Stadium was swinging
to the bopping sound,
but the fabulous Dixies
were the daddies of them all.
Across the ring they strutted
like court jesters:
zany Joe, sturdy Chris,
hefty Steve and clean-cut Brendan.
It was the wildest reception
I have ever seen at the venue.

Waiting to Go On

When I hear the five-minute call
for Orchestra and Beginners
I take my chair upstairs
and sit in the wings in my underpants,
my trousers over one arm.
I'm not in the first scene,
but I don't trust the Tannoy any more
after what happened the other night.
'If you're not coming on, Mr Williams,
that's all right with me,
but for God's sake don't come on late.'

They let the first Walking Gentleman go
after only one warning
just for lying down between the Acts.
They didn't bother auditioning the part,
they recast the suit
and I happened to have short arms.
It's cold sitting here night after night
with nothing over my knees,
but the suit belongs to the Company
and I don't want to be fined
for having poor creases.

Mirth

The lights come up, the stage is bare,
the audience goes on sitting there,

row upon row of gleaming teeth,
set in expressions of dutiful mirth

for something they have long since forgotten.
Someone has spilled an ice-cream cone

from the Balcony onto someone's head.
It trickles down over his forehead

and from there down into his lap.
We see the smile fade from his lips,

the lips fade from his mouth,
the mouth slowly wither from his teeth.

Now his jaw drops open on its tendons
and a look of horrified understanding dawns.

The urge to clap is irresistible.
He finds this is no longer possible.

Leakage

Muscle patterns that show satisfaction or delight
as opposed to a disingenuous smirk
have been identified by the Laboratory of Human Interaction
to provide more information about suicidal patients
who want to check themselves out of hospital
in order to take their own lives.

The best test for a genuine smile
is to look at the eyebrow and watch for skin droop.
The skin under the eyebrow is lowered only in genuine smiles.
Unhappy feelings show through false smiles
for about one third of a second
in what we term 'leakage'.

Everyone Knows This

Every object, every action,
a light suddenly switched on,
a door left open,
carries a hidden watermark
of joy or joylessness,
hope or hopelessness,
which might reveal itself
in the look on someone's face.

Children crying in the next door house,
young men going to work,
the saxophone solo
in 'I'm Gonna Be a Wheel Some Day',
are sorrowful or reassuring
depending on a smell of garlic
drifting up from downstairs,
or the sound of a horse race.

We live in a tiny place
where everything is attached
to something else, more precious.
Dog-barks, head-shakes,
unexpected knocks
bring tears to our eyes.
A box of Brillo pads
comes close to happiness.

The Sea

i.m. K.S.

When I am with you, I am a minute behind,
picking up pieces of coloured glass
and calling you back to me, 'Look . . .'

You have seen something new up ahead.
You don't look round. There you go,
scrambling over rocks on your way to the sea.

In My Absence

Provide a short piece of writing about your life.
It doesn't have to be a long, rambling account,
saying what you think it all means,
just something you could read out to our members,
or which could be read out in your absence.

Untitled

O tender two-note songs without refrains,
don't I remember you?
Haven't I waited till now
for you to come round once more,
holding out to me like hands
those frail, forgiving themes?

It makes me tremble to know
I wasted so many days.
My thirst for you
lies buried in the lake,
which reaches out to me hands I can't touch,
a life I can't drink from or break.

After the Writing Course

A few white plastic chairs
placed here and there
in writerly seclusion,
or huddling in pairs,
recall a life of excited
rivalry lived here
as recently as yesterday.
The lime tree has let fall
hundreds of little
floating contraptions,
which parade around the swimming pool
in great irregular crowds.
Out of habit, I note
how each individual
raft-like structure
has a mast and mainsail
which propel it confidently
towards an uncertain future.

Last Poem

I have put on a grotesque mask
to write these lines. I sit
staring at myself
in a mirror propped on my desk.

I hold up my head
like one of those Chinese lanterns
hollowed out of a pumpkin,
swinging from a broom.

I peer through the eye-holes
into that little lighted room
where a candle burns,
making me feel drowsy.

I must try not to spill the flame
wobbling in its pool of wax.
It sheds no light on the scene,
only shadows flickering up the walls.

In the narrow slit of my mouth
my tongue appears,
darting back and forth
behind the bars of my teeth.

I incline my head,
to try and catch what I am saying.
No sound emerges, only
the coming and going of my breath.